Snake

Chinese

Horoscope

2025

By
IChingHunFùyǒu FengShuisu

Table of Contents

Introduce

The character of people born in the year of the SNAKE

People born in this year speak less and have cute faces. Anyone who sees it is likely to be persistent and charming. Loved by others, speaks little, avoids gossip, and has good manners. People this year have never been in debt, and know how to save, but are sluggish. But being a thinker is beneficial. A wise and determined individual who does not abandon anything in the middle of the road. People born in the Year of the Snake trust first impressions, feelings, sympathy, advice, and other people's opinions. Incorporating the sixth sense into decision-making.

Even if he is a person who likes to talk less, when he has spoken, he often speaks exaggeratedly. Another is a good lie. No matter how big or small and survive every time. People born this year love to flirt and have sex, but not too nasty. So people come to fall in love with this year's man with a big head because they are romantic, very jealous, likes to have high expectations, wants to feel confident, and is always safe.

Strength:
You are a scholar who is intelligent and enjoys learning.

Weaknesses:
You're narcissistic and self-sufficient.

Love:
People born in this year have a lot of boyfriends. Because so much love must confront the chaos of love until it hurts. There is always a love that is so hot and flirtatious that it cannot keep up. Some people may not have a unique partnership with whom to demonstrate their charm. Old women and widows are buzzing, even though they are not attractive or attractive. Because your grace's style and eloquence It's so catchy, don't tell anyone Flirting extends to even the smallest snake people. However, if someone is already a fan, I can assure you that I am the most envious. Do

not allow anyone to interfere. Most importantly, enjoy being selfish and impatient.

Suitable Career:
Because Snakes are fire-elemental, those born in the year of the Snake should pursue a career related to fire, such as opening a shop for electrical or electronic devices such as radios, and televisions, or selling electrical appliances. Open a gas station, or pursue a career that necessitates specific skills, such as being a speaker, critic, judge, prosecutor, teacher, writer, politician, journalist, beautician, photographer, makeup artist, or model. Modeling, selling artificial plants, trees, and flowers, fortune telling in various fields, the military, and law enforcement are all suitable professions for those born in the year of the Snake.

Year of the SNAKE (Gold) | (1941) & (2001)

"The Snake in hibernation" is a person born in the year of the SNAKE at the age of 84 years (1941) and 24 years (2001)

Overview

For senior people in this age group, the most important thing at this time is to take care of your health, both physical and mental. For physical health, you must focus on eating hygienic food and doing light exercise regularly. You should also see a doctor for regular check-ups and get enough sleep. For mental health, you must learn to let go of your children. If your children have problems, let them handle the problems themselves. Don't be too fussy. The best thing is to give your children blessings. It will be good for them and yourself. In addition, at the beginning of the year, you should find an opportunity to worship the Tai Sui deity to ward off bad luck. If it is inconvenient to travel by yourself, you can bring a set of offerings bought from the company or store to perform the "Kaleow" ceremony. Take the set of paper offerings and brush them from your head down to your body 12 times. Then, leave it with your children or close friends to place at the place provided by the temple so that the Tai Sui deity can take care of your destiny and ward off bad luck. For young people in this age group, this year the auspicious stars will spread their rays, allowing you to find patrons and help you, and help you gain wisdom to help solve various problems. Your work will also change in a good direction and you will progress. But since there are bad stars that are harassing you during the year, which will cause accidents, you cannot be careless while working and traveling because you may get injured. In addition, there will be problems with illnesses that threaten you. You should be careful and not drink alcohol to the point of losing your senses.

In terms of love, you will encounter a third party. Your relationship during the year will be rather bumpy and not smooth. In addition, your birth year conflicts with your birth year. At the beginning of the year, you should find an opportunity to pay respect and ask for blessings from Tai Sui to ward off bad luck and reduce the severity.

Career and Business

This year, since your horoscope falls in the unlucky year, you should be careful of conflicts in your organization or with people close to you. Even though you will receive blessings from the auspicious stars, they will only help you to some extent. However, you will have to rely on your intelligence and diligence in developing new skills and knowledge to overcome problems and obstacles in your career. If you are still studying, you should be determined to reach your goal. The months when your career and education will change for the better are: 2nd Chinese month (March 5 – April 3), 6th Chinese month (July 7 – August 6), 7th Chinese month (August 7 – September 6), and 8th Chinese month (September 7 – October 7). As for investments, you should be careful of dishonest partners' embezzlement or account manipulation. Therefore, you should be more careful during the following periods because you will encounter many obstacles, including the 1st Chinese month (February 3 - March 4), the 3rd Chinese month (April 4 - May 4), the 9th Chinese month (October 8 - November 6), and the 10th Chinese month (November 7 - December 6). During the aforementioned periods, please remember that forgetting yourself, lacking respect, and being too arrogant will cause harm to yourself. You should also be careful not to be fooled or taken advantage of by others. When making documents or contracts, you should be careful not to be selfish because you may suffer later. As for starting a new job, entering into a joint venture, and investing during these periods, you should avoid them.

Financial

This year, your finances are not good. Your income is low, but your expenses are on time. There may also be unexpected current expenses intervening at times. As for the money from windfalls, you will lose more than you gain. Therefore, do not be greedy. It may cause your liquidity to be in crisis. Therefore, this year, you should spend thriftily and take good care of your liquidity, especially during the months when your finances will be low and sluggish and unexpected expenses may occur: Chinese month 1 (February 3 - March 4), Chinese month 3 (April 4 - May 4), Chinese month 9 (October 8 - November 6), and Chinese month 10 (November 7 - December 6). During these periods, you should not gamble, lend money to others, or sign financial guarantees. Do not be greedy or you will easily fall victim to fraud. Do not invest in illegal businesses. The months when your finances will flow smoothly are the 2nd Chinese month (March 5 – April 3), the 6th Chinese month (July 7 – August 6), the 7th Chinese month (August 7 – September 6), and the 8th Chinese month (September 7 – October 7).

Family

This year, your family will not be smooth. You should be careful about safety because there is a possibility that you or your family members may suffer injuries and health problems of the elders in the family. Also, do not get involved in conflicts between friends, especially those that may lead to legal cases. You should also stay away from friends who like to invite you to have fun and get drunk on alcohol and vices. The months when your family will face problems and conflicts are the 1st Chinese month (February 3 - March 4), the 3rd Chinese month (April 4 - May 4), the 9th Chinese month (October 8 - November 6), and the 10th Chinese month (November 7 - December 6). You should be careful of juniors or servants in the house who may cause trouble for the whole family. Also, be careful of losing valuables, being damaged, or falling victim to fraud.

Love

This year, love and relationships are difficult to predict. Because your mood is often irritated. You tend to dislike or annoy things you see. If someone criticizes you, you will immediately respond violently. Therefore, you should be mindful of your emotions. Otherwise, the relationship that has been going on will only break. Especially during the months when your love is quite fragile and arguments may easily occur, such as the 1st Chinese month (February

3 - March 4), the 3rd Chinese month (April 4 - May 4), the 9th Chinese month (October 8 - November 6), and the 10th Chinese month (November 7 - December 6). You should avoid triggers that will cause arguments. If you know that you are angry, calm down first and then talk to each other with reason. You should not be sarcastic by going to entertainment venues, which will only add fuel to the fire and bring trouble back.

Health

This year, young people should be careful of alcohol, e-cigarettes, or other addictive substances, which will bring trouble and illness. In addition, you are likely to get injured while working with tools and machines, as well as using vehicles on the road. The months when you should take care of your health and exercise regularly are the 1st Chinese month (February 3 – March 4), the 3rd Chinese month (April 4 – May 4), the 9th Chinese month (October 8 – November 6), and the 10th Chinese month (November 7 – December 6). For seniors, this year you need to be more strict about taking care of yourself. You need to make sure your food is hygienic. You should take the medicine prescribed by the doctor on time. You should get enough rest and see a doctor for regular checkups.

Year of the SNAKE (Water) | (1953) & (2013)

" The SNAKE in the grass " is a person born in the year of the SNAKE at the age of 72 years (1953) and 12 years (2013)

Overview

For young people in this age group, overall academic results will be supported by auspicious stars to progress well. However, the person should always be diligent in reviewing lessons. If there is anything you do not understand, ask your teachers. This will help your academic results reach your intended goal. Since this year overlaps with your birth year, some things will cause chaos: allergies, frequent colds, and unexpected accidents. You should also be careful with your manners towards elders and teachers. Do not be arrogant or show off your skills, which will lead to disaster. Therefore, at the beginning of the year, parents should take their children to pay homage to the Tai Sui deity (the deity who protects destiny) to alleviate disasters, turn bad events into good things, and help dissolve various disasters.

For senior people in this age group, this year it will be difficult to avoid problems and obstacles. You should be careful of unexpected events that may occur, such as losses or damages from accidents, health problems, especially hidden diseases. You should also be careful about your diet. You should take care of and control sugar, fat, and saltiness because they will cause illnesses to follow. In addition, there is a chance that you will suffer from mourning for your elder relatives. Since this year overlaps with your birth year, At the beginning of the year, you should find time to pay homage to Tai Sui (the god who protects your destiny) to alleviate your misfortunes, change your problems to be lighter, and help dispel various misfortunes.

Career and Business

The career and business of the person is in chaos. This year is a good time for you to find an heir or someone close to you to help you continue your work. You should gradually reduce your work or put it down because bad stars are moving into your horoscope house. This will result in conflicts in your organization and many problems and obstacles. Therefore, you should use your long-term experience to solve the problems that arise. Especially during the months when your career or business will be stuck and have problems, such as the 1st Chinese month (February 3 - March 4), the 3rd Chinese month (April 4 - May 4), the 9th Chinese month (October 8 - November 6), and the 10th Chinese month (November 7 - December 6). Be careful of your subordinates or workers in your organization making mistakes that cause damage. Also, entering into shares or joint ventures will cause corruption and create problems and suffering for the youth. Although the intellectual power from the Boon Chiang star will help promote your studies, you should be careful of temptations that will lead you astray. Therefore, parents or guardians are asked to take good care of children because children are still inexperienced, making it easy for them to be led in the wrong direction. The months in which the studies and careers of the person in both cycles of life will change for the better are the 2nd Chinese month (March 5 - April 3), the 6th Chinese month (July 7 - August 6), the 7th Chinese month (August 7 - September 6), and the 8th Chinese month (September 7 - October 7).

Financial

Your finances are moderate. Direct income from salary or sales of goods and services still flows normally. However, money from gambling must be more careful. Because it is an unlucky year, there will be unexpected disasters and loss of property. You should also be careful of your subordinates (servants or subordinates) causing damage and loss of property. Therefore, you should prepare liquidity to cope, especially during the months when your finances will be interrupted and lack liquidity, which are Chinese month 1 (February 3 - March 4), Chinese month 3 (April 4 - May 4), Chinese month 9 (October 8 - November 6), and Chinese month 10 (November 7 - December 6). Do not gamble, do not lend money, or sign as guarantors. Do not be greedy or you will easily fall victim to fraud. Do not expose valuables to the temptation to prevent danger from thieves. The months when your finances will flow smoothly are the 2nd Chinese month (5 March – 3 April), the 6th Chinese month (7 July – 6 August), the 7th Chinese month (7 August – 6 September), and the 8th Chinese month (7 September – 7 October).

Family

This year, the family horoscope is not very good because evil stars are orbiting to harass and stare, causing people in the house to often have conflicts and arguments. In addition, you should take care of safety and accidents that may occur. You should also be careful about mourning for elders, which will cause the house to lack peace, especially during the 1st Chinese

Month (February 3 - March 4), the 3rd Chinese Month (April 4 - May 4), 9th Chinese Month (October 8 - November 6), and 10th Chinese Month (November 7 - December 6). Another thing that the person must be careful about is that younger people in the house have arguments with neighbors. In addition, you should keep up with news on social media about scams by criminals to know how to protect yourself and your family. The electrical system and appliances that are firmly fixed in the house should be checked to be in good condition and not damaged because they may fall and harm family members. In addition, when traveling near or far, you must not be careless and always be careful of accidents.

Love

For senior people, this year is suitable for taking your partner on a pilgrimage to worship the gods and spirits, as well as participating in merit-making ceremonies. This will help clear your mind and resolve many matters for the better. However, you should be careful during the following months when love can easily lead to arguments and disputes: 1st Chinese month (February 3 – March 4), 3rd Chinese month (April 4 – May 4), 9th Chinese month (October 8 – November 6), and the 10th Chinese month (November 7 – December 6). For senior people, be careful not to interfere in other people's family matters. You should conduct yourself well and be patient. Do not be picky or criticize your children. You should reduce your loud criticism because it will only cause arguments. Do not be gullible and listen to gossip. You must have a strong mind, which will make your children love you. As for young people, you must be humble and modest. You may demand attention and love from adults. Adults should set aside time to understand and gradually guide you on what should be done. Do not take your emotions out on work or outside matters with children. Then the children will behave better.

Health
For the elderly, the health horoscope this year is not good. Be careful when using tools or machinery as it may cause injury. Walking on

high and low ground may cause tripping and falling. Traveling far to a strange place, be careful of unexpected events. In addition, both horoscopes of both age groups are likely to mourn relatives, especially during the 1st Chinese month (February 3 - March 4), the 3rd Chinese month (April 4 - May 4), the 9th Chinese month (October 8 - November 6), and the 10th Chinese month (November 7 - December 6). For young people, be careful of accidents from playing or traveling to strange places, especially dangers from water.

Year of the SNAKE (Fire) | (1965)

" The snake comes out of the cave. " is a person born in the year of the SNAKE at the age of 60 years (1965)

Overview

For the 60-year-old snake, since this year falls in the same year as your birth year, your birth year is classified as one of the zodiac clashes. In addition, there will be an evil star in your horoscope house, which will cause unexpected losses. You can solve this problem from the beginning of the year by buying things you like, electrical appliances, gold, or other things. You should also be careful about health problems and be careful about being obsessed with vices, which will cause negative consequences. You will also have to face conflicts and chaos throughout the year. However, because your horoscope house has auspicious stars to help, your misfortunes will be alleviated. However, you should not use emotions in your work and business decisions this year. In terms of health, be careful of chronic diseases that flare up and disappear. They will take a long time to heal and be careful of hidden diseases. You should also be careful of accidents both while working and traveling. This year, avoid attending funerals, whether you are the chairman or vice chairman of the ceremony, traveling to send the body to the cemetery, or even eating at funerals. If you can avoid it, you should avoid it. At the beginning of the year, you should find time to pay respect to the Buddha and deities. Paying homage to the Tai Sui deity (the deity who protects your destiny for the year) will help you overcome the clashing energy and find only auspicious things and good fortune. In addition, you should find an opportunity to practice meditation as time permits, which will help reduce health problems. You should also plan your work and business carefully and keep up with changes to reduce problems that will cause you to worry later.

Career and Business

This year, the person's career and business are not going well. Human resource management is likely to have problems. Beware of envious people, especially during the months when the career star is low and your work is obstructed and has problems, namely the 1st Chinese month (February 3 – March 4), the 3rd Chinese month (April 4 – May 4), the 9th Chinese month (October 8 – November 6), and the 10th Chinese month (November 7 – December 6). During these months, the person must beware of ill-wishers who intend to backstab and slander. In terms of work this year, it is important that you listen to your coworkers' opinions and manage your work with fairness and transparency to show your coworkers and subordinates that they are being treated fairly. This is one way to reduce conflicts and solve critical points in your work. In addition, making legal contracts during these months must be done carefully and thoroughly. Beware of being deceived. Also, beware of subordinates or subordinates making mistakes that cause damage. The months when work and business are in a prosperous direction are the 2nd Chinese month (March 5 – April 3), the 6th Chinese month (July 7 – August 6), the 7th Chinese month (August 7 – September 6), and the 8th Chinese month (September 7 – October 7). Many investments are in a good position with a future, causing you to receive a usable return. However, you should start looking for an heir or assistant to take care of or continue the work so that you can choose the best and most appropriate channel for operations and moving forward.

Financial

This year, your financial luck is uncertain because it is affected by the clashing power of the year. Although you may receive some windfall income during the year, there will be unexpected expenses that will interfere and cause you to lose your money. A solution for some women is to buy a gold necklace or gold bracelet to wear or buy electrical appliances or other necessary items that you like. Although it may seem extravagant, it is considered a solution to the bad luck of losing money since the beginning of the year. However, it would be better if you save up for anything that is not necessary. Especially during the months when your finances will be stuck and lack liquidity, you should save up and tighten your belt, which are the months of the 1st Chinese month (February 3 - March 4), the 3rd Chinese month (April 4 - May 4), the 9th Chinese month (October 8 - November 6), and the 10th Chinese month (November 7 - December 6). Do not gamble, do not lend money to others, or be a financial guarantee. Do not do immoral businesses, copyright infringement, or illegal businesses. Be careful not to fall into the trap of being lured by the lure of money. If you are greedy, you may lose everything. The months when your finances will flow smoothly are the 2nd Chinese month (March 5 – April 3), the 6th Chinese month (July 7 – August 6), the 7th Chinese month (August 7 – September 6), and the 8th Chinese month (September 7 – October 7).

Family
This year, your family's horoscope is stuck. You should make merit and do good deeds to help break up the chaotic energy and clear it up. However, you should be careful of accidents that may happen to family members and be careful of juniors in the family who may cause trouble in the family, especially during the 1st Chinese month (February 3 – March 4), the 3rd Chinese month (April 4 – May 4), the 9th Chinese month (October 8 – November 6), and the 10th Chinese month (November 7 – December 6). Also, be careful of conflicts and arguments among family members. Be careful of losing valuables, being damaged, or

becoming a victim of fraud. Do not get involved in conflicts between friends, especially disputes that involve lawsuits. You should also avoid relatives who like to cheat, who may secretly bite or harm you, causing you trouble.

Love

Since the first half of the year will be smooth, the second half of the year will be affected by conflicting powers. Therefore, during bad times, you should control your emotions. Do not vent your frustration on your lover or close people. You should be patient with your feelings to maintain peace in your home. In addition to being considerate of the other person's feelings, it also helps maintain the love of those who have been together for a long time. Especially during the 1st Chinese Month (February 3 - March 4), the 3rd Chinese Month (April 4 - May 4), the 10th Chinese Month (October 8 - November 6), and the Chinese New Year (November 7 - December 6), you must be careful of arguing about small matters that become big matters. Do not interfere with other people's husbands and wives and do not be easily influenced by gossip and slander your partner. You should also avoid going to entertainment venues that offer services. Be careful of falling for children or being pursued by children, which may cause arguments with your real lover at home.

Health

This year, your health is not smooth. This is because, during the year, you will experience misfortune from the evil stars that will affect your health in terms of lack of self-control, and easily becoming obsessed with vices such as alcohol, women, or drugs. Therefore, you should take good care of your health and control your mind. Be careful of liver disease, heart disease, stomach disease, intestinal disease, frequent headaches, and accidents, especially in the following months: the 1st Chinese month (February 3 - March 4), the 3rd Chinese month (April 4 - May 4), the 9th Chinese month (October 8 - November 6), and the 10th Chinese month (November 7 - December 6). During these times, be extra careful of accidents from work, using tools, machines, and traveling. Be careful of getting sick from food poisoning.

Year of the SNAKE (Earth) | (1977)

" Snakes in rivers and canals" is a person born in the year of the SNAKE at the age of 48 years (1977)

Overview

For the Snake horoscope in this age group, this year is a criterion that must be considered before stepping forward because your birth year is classified as another zodiac sign that clashes. Therefore, you will encounter troubles and chaos that are hard to avoid. Many activities will not be as smooth and easy as you hope. Although the horoscope house shows auspicious stars orbiting to help, it only helps a part of it. For many other important parts, you still have to take care of and help yourself. Your work and business are places where you have to be patient and tolerant, and you have to be calm and careful in responding to problems and obstacles. Because if you explode with emotion, it will only make things worse and harder to solve. Also, be careful of the underlings in the dark corner who are trying to hurt or slander you and cause you trouble. In terms of finances, be careful of economic fluctuations that will affect your liquidity. Therefore, you should prepare both funds and an emergency backup plan in advance. This will help ease the situation from serious to light. In terms of family, be careful of unexpected bad news, including health problems. Be careful of silent diseases that appear to threaten you and make you worried. Therefore, this year, if you feel unwell or feel something unusual in your body, you should not be complacent. You should see a doctor immediately for diagnosis and treatment. Also, when it falls in a year that coincides with your birth year, At the beginning of the year, the person with a horoscope should find time to pay respect and ask for blessings from Tai Sui (the god who protects destiny) so that he can help alleviate and eliminate the misfortunes that will affect him this year.

Career and Business

For work and business this year, you will have to try twice as hard to achieve what you hope for because you will have to face many problems and obstacles. Therefore, please use your mind to solve problems carefully. You should not make any decisions hastily because mistakes may occur. You should check carefully before you proceed. You should also closely manage your work, and build and strengthen good relationships with all those involved in the work system, especially during the months when your work will be hindered and have problems, such as the 1st Chinese month (February 3 - March 4), the 3rd Chinese month (April 4 - May 4), the 9th Chinese month (October 8 - November 6), and the 10th Chinese month (November 7 - December 6). Be careful of mistakes in your work, conflicts in your management, and detailed consideration of contracts to avoid obligations that you cannot escape later. You may also find a partner who commits accounting fraud or an economic crisis that causes losses. The months when your work will change in a better direction are the 2nd Chinese month (March 5 – April 3), the 6th Chinese month (July 7 – August 6), the 7th Chinese month (August 7 – September 6) and the 8th Chinese month (September 7 – October 7).

Financial

This year, your finances will be in a state of loss, income will not be smooth, and there may be unexpected current expenses. Therefore, you should save anything that you can save first to ease your liquidity burden. You should stop hoping for gambling that you were lucky this year, especially during the months when your finances are low. This will cause your finances to be stuck and sluggish, namely, the 1st Chinese month (February 3 – March 4), the 3rd Chinese month (April 4 – May 4), the 9th Chinese month (October 8 – November 6), and the 10th Chinese month (November 7 – December 6). Do not gamble, do not lend money to others or sign as a financial guarantee, and do not do illegal business. The months when your financial luck is bright are the 2nd Chinese month (5 March – 3 April), the

6th Chinese month (July 7 – August 6), the 7th Chinese month (August 7 – September 6), and the 8th Chinese month (September 7 – October 7).

Family

This year, the family horoscope of this person is not smooth because it is affected by the clashing power. In addition, the horoscope house is also being targeted and harassed by evil stars, which will affect the safety and health problems of the people in the house. There are also problems of arguing in the house or with neighbors. Therefore, you should avoid prolonging the situation. Use calmness to resolve the conflict. Do not use the heart of a gangster to respond. The matter will then be calm. Especially during the months when problems and arguments in your family are easily caused, such as the 1st Chinese month (February 3 - March 4), the 3rd Chinese month (April 4 - May 4), the 9th Chinese month (October 8 - November 6), and the 10th Chinese month (November 7 - December 6), you should be more careful about accidents in the house.

Avoid the cause of the argument. You should also be careful of the dark dangers of thieves. In addition, do not get involved in the disputes of your friends, especially about legal cases. Do not interfere in your friends' matters.

Love

This year, love will be mixed with both good and bad. Sometimes you will feel that your lover is acting in a way that is irritating, irritating, or provoking you, which can easily lead to arguments. Therefore, what you should do this year is to give your lover more time and forgive them for some things that have happened in the past. Because of the unlucky year, there will often be chaotic events that will make your mind restless, especially during the 1st Chinese month (February 3 – March 4), the 3rd Chinese month (April 4 – May 4), the 9th Chinese month (October 8 – November 6), and the 10th Chinese month (November 7 – December 6), when you should avoid verbal conflicts and not listen to others' instigations. In addition, avoid getting involved with other people's spouses. You should try to control your emotions and words, or end it by finding a quiet place. This will help reduce the rift and help preserve your love. Importantly, you should not go to entertainment venues because you may suffer from loss of property and illness.

Health

This year is not very good because there is an inauspicious constellation that is focusing on your health base. It will affect illness, accidents, and unexpected things. Especially during the months when you should pay close attention to your health, which are the 1st Chinese month (February 3 - March 4), the 3rd Chinese month (April 4 - May 4), the 9th Chinese month (October 8 - November 6) and the 10th Chinese month (November 7 - December 6). You should be more careful of accidents while working, using tools and machines, and traveling because you are likely to suffer injuries and bleeding. In addition, you should pay more attention to hygiene in eating and drinking. Also, be careful of infectious diseases and hidden diseases that may threaten you.

Year of the SNAKE (Wood) | (1989)

"The Lucky Snake " is a person born in the year of the SNAKE at the age of 36 years (1989)

Overview

For the people born in the year of the Snake, this year falls in the year that is directly on top of the birth year, which is considered to be a violation of the Tai Sui deity. Therefore, it is a criterion that must be watched out for. Must work under uncertainty. If you are mindful and not rash, you will progress. Do not be afraid of losing your job or being hungry. However, you should improve your interpersonal skills at both the upper and lower levels. Also, you must constantly increase your new skills and knowledge to keep up with the changes. Do not isolate yourself by avoiding society because that is like limiting your progress and causing your relationships with others to stop. However, this year you should use your intelligence, ability, and diligence to help the group and work together as a team. This way, you will not lose the opportunity to advance to the next level. Or even if you want to expand your work or business, you will receive cooperation and help. Because this year, if you do a lot, you have a chance to earn a lot of money. But you cannot succeed alone. You need to receive support and encouragement from people around you. However, in terms of your work or business, this year is often not smooth. Therefore, you should proceed with your work carefully. You should not make hasty decisions because it will have negative effects. This year, your work and business will have problems and obstacles that harass you. But fortunately, there are auspicious stars to help. When adding and subtracting, there is still a positive result. Therefore, please do not be discouraged. If you add determination and develop other additional skills, there will be progress waiting. In terms of financial luck, this year is not very good. You should avoid gambling and risky businesses. Do not invest in businesses that are at risk of the law. Importantly, you are likely to experience a liquidity crisis. Therefore, you should plan your finances and save money for emergencies. In terms of family, this year you should spend more time with your family members to help restore relationships. Good communication and conversation will bring peace to the family. In addition, at the beginning of the year, you should find time to worship and ward off bad luck to the Tai Sui deity (the guardian deity of the year) to help ease many things from serious to light.

Career and Business

This year, your career and business will progress because you will have a patron in your horoscope and will receive auspicious energy from auspicious stars. Therefore, it is a good opportunity to create work, expand your trading base, and increase sales. If you are more diligent and persistent, and constantly add knowledge and strengthen your relationships with people around you, you will be able to overcome any problems and obstacles. The months in which you will have luck in your career and investments are the 2nd Chinese month (March 5 – April 3), the 6th Chinese month (July 7 – August 6), the 7th Chinese month (August 7 – September 6), and the 8th Chinese month (September 7 – October 7). The months in which your career will encounter problems are the 1st Chinese month (February 3 – March 4), the 3rd Chinese month (April 4 – May 4), the 9th Chinese month (October 8 – November 6), and the 10th Chinese month (November 7 – December 6). Executing various documents and contracts Regarding work during this period, be careful of being deceived. Also, be careful of mistakes and damages that may occur in work and conflicts between people. For joint ventures this year, it is a criterion to watch out for because of the power of the bad stars surrounding the horoscope house. In working, joint ventures, or various investments, do not be fooled by the beautiful illusions that others bring dreamy projects to lure with good profits because in the name of "business", there is no free thing in the world. When there is profit, there is also a chance of loss. In addition, in work, you should communicate clearly with others before starting to do it. This will save you from wasting time going back to fix mistakes and damages.

Financial

This year's finances are a stormy sign. Although direct income from salary or sales of goods and services still flows normally, there will be unexpectedly large expenses. If you hope for money from gambling, there is a high risk. Some people may choose to solve the bad luck of losing money by buying things that they like and are expensive since the beginning of the year, such as buying electrical appliances that they want or gold necklaces or gold bracelets, etc., which can alleviate the danger of losing money. However, you should be careful during the months when your finances will be low and you will experience a lack of liquidity, which are the 1st Chinese month (February 3 - March 4), the 3rd Chinese month (April 4 - May 4), the 9th Chinese month (October 8 - November 6), and the 10th Chinese month (November 7 - December 6). Gambling and gambling are prohibited. Lending money to others or signing financial guarantees is prohibited. And doing illegal business is prohibited. The months when your finances will flow smoothly are the 2nd Chinese month (March 5 – April 3), the 6th

Chinese month (July 7 – August 6), the 7th Chinese month (August 7 – September 6), and the 8th Chinese month (September 7 – October 7).

Family

Your family's horoscope is not good. Therefore, at the beginning of the year, you should find time to worship the gods pray for blessings, and ward off bad luck from Tai Sui. This will help protect you and your family members and alleviate their suffering. Since your birth year is considered a clashing year, this year, you will encounter bad stars that will harass your family, which will cause problems with government agencies or legal disputes. In particular, the months when your family will encounter problems and conflicts are the 1st Chinese month (February 3 – March 4), the 3rd Chinese month (April 4 – May 4), the 9th Chinese month (October 8 – November 6), and the 10th Chinese month (November 7 – December 6). Be careful of arguments in the house. Be careful of arguments with neighbors. Be careful of accidents that may happen to family members that may cause injuries. Be careful of valuables that may be lost, damaged, or become a victim of fraud. As for your relatives' horoscope, this year is a year of uncertainty. What you will encounter will be both good and bad. You should be careful of both your words and actions. Sometimes, you may just be joking or joking. But friends who are teased or listened to by you feel that they are being looked down upon and may unknowingly cause themselves a dark danger.

Love

This year, the love horoscope of this person seems to be not in order. There are often arguments that make love not smooth. And there is often a third party that interferes, causing misunderstandings. If love lacks patience and tolerance, it can reach a breaking point. Therefore, you should be considerate, put yourself in other people's shoes, and consider the heirs that you have to take responsibility for taking care of. Especially during the months when your love is quite fragile and conflicts are likely to occur, such as the 1st Chinese month (February 3 - March 4), the 3rd Chinese month (April 4 - May 4), the 9th Chinese month (October 8 - November 6), and the 10th Chinese month (November 7 - December 6), when your mind must be strong. Do not be easily influenced by gossip or provocative words. It will cause unnecessary arguments. Avoid getting involved with other people's husbands and wives. Avoid going to entertainment venues that may cause illnesses and cause you trouble.

Health

This year, your health is quite weak. You will get sick easily. Be careful of illnesses that may occur due to overindulgence. In particular, you should be careful about your eating and drinking habits. Avoid foods that are cold or have a cold element, such as winter melon, watermelon, ice, and various frozen foods. Drinking alcohol should be limited. Be mindful when going out to social events. Do not let alcohol take you away and ruin you. In addition, you should be careful of accidents both at work and while traveling. In particular, the months when your health will cause problems are the 1st Chinese month (February 3 – March 4), the 3rd Chinese month (April 4 – May 4), the 9th Chinese month (October 8 – November 6), and the 10th Chinese month (November 7 – December 6). You should be especially mindful. Be careful of injuries, bleeding, and illnesses that may leave you bedridden.

Chinese Astrology Horoscope for Each Month

Month 12 in the Dragon Year (5 Jan 25 - 2 Feb 25)

This month, your life path is like coming across a steep mountain, difficult to climb up. Therefore, it is a time when many things are hanging on uncertainty. Even though good opportunities are approaching, you often fail and try not to reach them in the right direction. In terms of your career and business, you will encounter a barrier. Talking too much will cause damage. In any operation during this period, you must be honest, fair, and transparent. Otherwise, your business partners or customers will lose faith in and trust you. In the end, your business will reach a dead end. You should also be careful of dishonest subordinates, embezzlement, or account fraud. In addition, you must be more careful when conducting legal contracts. Be careful not to be tricked until you have to pay. There are important things you should be careful of this month: Be careful of people close to you who harm or secretly harm you. Be careful of dishonest subordinates and partners. Another thing you should be aware of is that when accepting work, do not just promise. Instead, you should consider whether you can do it on time. If you cannot, do not promise or sign the contract in advance, or your reputation will be damaged.

This salary horoscope is a criterion that if you do a lot, you will get a lot. If you are lazy, you will get a little money. However, you should be careful of money from luck. If you are greedy, you may lose money instead. Therefore, it is better to avoid taking risks.

The family is peaceful, but during this period, joint ventures and investments that require some dependence on each other should be avoided. Be careful of being considerate, you may have to come to terms with it later.

As for love, it is moderate. Even if your lover does not hate you, if you are too persistent or picky with the other person to the point of being annoying, it is not good. Therefore, talking, asking questions, and taking care of each other should be at a moderate level.

As for health, you may get sick sometimes because you forget to take care of your health. During this period, you should be careful of food poisoning.

Support Days: 4 Jan., 8 Jan., 12 Jan., 16 Jan., 20 Jan., 24 Jan., 28 Jan.
Lucky Days: 3 Jan., 15 Jan., 27 Jan.
Misfortune Days: 6 Jan., 18 Jan., 30 Jan.
Bad Days: 9 Jan., 21 Jan.

Month 1 in the Snake Year (3 Feb 25 - 4 Mar 25)
Since this year is the same as the birth year and is experiencing a clash of power, at the beginning of the year, such as this month, people born in the Year of the Snake should find time to pay homage to Tai Sui (the god of destiny) to ward off bad luck. In addition, there are many bad stars in the horoscope house. This year, there will be frequent losses of property. Some people therefore like to buy expensive items that they like from the beginning of the year to resolve the bad omen

of losing property so that they do not have to lose more property.

As for the salary, it is not good, so gambling and taking risks are prohibited. Do not lend money to others. Do not invest in businesses that are at risk of breaking the law. You should carefully manage your income and expenses and prepare to save money to help solve problems in times of crisis or emergency.

As for work, you will face challenges. Be careful of problems in personnel management and problems in contacting customers or business partners who may die more. In addition, when making legal contracts during this period, be careful of hidden details that will put you at a disadvantage. Therefore, you should focus on your work and be more careful. Avoid triggers that will cause problems to survive safely. You must also closely supervise your work or business. If problems appear, solve them immediately and do not let them escalate. And do not interfere with the work and responsibilities of others.

The family's horoscope lacks peace. You must be careful of the health and safety of people in the house. Be careful of valuables being lost or stolen. And be careful of relatives who come to bother you about money.

In terms of love, there will be new friendships, but this time it is not the right person. So you should not rush to make a decision.

Health is not very good. Be careful of food poisoning. So you should always take strict care of your hygiene. Also, be careful of injuries on the road or falls that will affect your bones.

Support Days: 1 Feb., 5 Feb., 9 Feb., 13 Feb., 17 Feb., 21 Feb., 25 Feb.
Lucky Days: 8 Feb., 20 Feb.
Misfortune Days: 11 Feb., 23 Feb.
Bad Days: 2 Feb., 14 Feb., 26 Feb.

Month 2 in the Snake Year (6 Mar 25 - 5 Apr 25)
This month, your horoscope is on the rise because you are receiving auspicious rays from good stars who are supporting and promoting

you. Therefore, during this period, whether it is work that you are responsible for, business, or education, you will see good progress and prosperity. What you should do this month is to find time to visit and greet those you have to contact, and diligently create and strengthen good relationships with people around you, including customers, business partners, people you have to contact, including your boss, and subordinates. On the other hand, you should collect capital to wait for the right time and opportunity to start investing again.

Your financial luck is fair. You still have income from salary and sales that you can use, but for unexpected money, it is better not to take risks. You still have to save money during this period to survive the crisis.

In terms of work, this month you will meet a sponsor. This is a good time to increase your work, make sales, expand your production and trading base, and you have to check the details carefully. Don't forget that you have to be patient in everything you do. Don't let your emotions control you. Most importantly, you should take care of your work and responsibilities as best you can. Do not interfere with others' work. Collaboration or investment will yield good returns.

Your family horoscope this month is peaceful. There will be good news or opportunities to receive wealth. Relatives are good. You will receive support and assistance.

As for love, it has a chance to be fulfilled. Just show courage to get to know each other or tell your feelings.

In terms of health, even if you are healthy, you may get a little sick. See a doctor, take medicine, and rest, and you will recover normally.

Support Days: 1 Mar, 5 Mar., 9 Mar., 13 Mar., 17 Mar., 21 Mar., 25 Mar., 29 Mar.
Lucky Days: 9 Mar, 21 Mar.
Misfortune Days: 7 Mar, 19 Mar., 31 Mar.
Bad Days: 10 Mar, 22 Mar.

Month 3 in the Snake Year (4 Apr 25 - 4 May 25)

This month, the horoscope of those born in the year of the Snake shows a group of bad stars invading the horoscope house, like bad karma hitting you repeatedly, causing your horoscope to fall dramatically. Problems and obstacles will appear in your work, business, and finances. You should be careful. What you should do this month is to take care of your safety first. Do not go near an environment that may cause trouble. This month, your financial luck will be in the position of losing money. Do not spend by creating debts and be careful of debtors who may suffer bad debts. In addition, there will be unexpected expenses, causing you to face financial problems. However, if you have a good plan and budget in advance, you will be able to get through this period.

In terms of work, be careful of conflicts at work. You will encounter silent protests from your subordinates. You should be careful of envious people who are trying to find ways to bully you. Therefore, you should use good human relations skills, know how to compromise, use your mind to solve problems, and avoid using emotions. When making documents or contracts, be careful of being cheated and taken advantage of. As for starting a new job or investing, you should refrain for now.

In terms of family, be careful of safety in the home and health problems of family members. There may be a danger of mourning for an elder relative. Be careful of valuables being damaged. Lost or some may fall victim to scammers.

For bad love, singles beware of being cheated, and couples beware of arguments.

Health is still not favorable, you must be careful of injuries from accidents and food poisoning.

Support Days: 2 Apr., 6 Apr., 10 Apr., 14 Apr., 18 Apr., 22 Apr., 26 Apr., 30 Apr.
Lucky Days: 9 Apr., 21 Apr.
Misfortune Days: 12 Apr., 24 Apr.
Bad Days: 3 Apr., 15 Apr., 27 Apr.

Month 4 in the Snake Year (5 May 25 - 4 Jun 25)
This month, your horoscope will experience half good and half bad. For your business, you must be careful that you may be tricked or drugged to cause problems and troubles later. What you should do this month is to keep some of your work a secret and to protect yourself. Do not put yourself at risk of conflicts, especially in cases that are at risk of becoming a lawsuit. It is best to know how to protect yourself. However, starting a new job, entering into a joint venture, and investing in various things should be avoided for now.

This month, your income and expenses will be low. Therefore, save first to have liquidity. It is better than spending too much and causing your finances to go into the red and having problems later. You must also be careful of unexpected expenses. Therefore, you should save up and cut out unnecessary expenses. Gambling, vices, and various forms of gambling should be avoided because they will cause you to lose even more money.

In terms of your family, you should be careful that your subordinates cause arguments. Be careful that valuable property is lost or stolen. You must also take care of your family members' health. You may fall ill and have to go to the hospital. Be careful of accidents while traveling. This month, do not get involved in other people's family matters because it may cause problems later. Your family will be peaceful and your family members will be in harmony and love each other.

In terms of love, it will be smooth and bright. During this period, you will have the opportunity to travel with your partner, whether it is for a vacation or to make merit, which will be a memorable time.

In terms of health, during this period, be careful of injuries from machinery or accidents while traveling.

Support Days: 4 May, 8 May., 12 May., 16 May., 20 May., 24 May., 28 May.
Lucky Days: 3 May., 15 May., 27 May.

Misfortune Days: 6 May., 18 May., 30 May.
Bad Days: 9 May., 21 May.

Month 5 in the Snake Year (5 Jun 25 - 6 Jul 25)

This month, your horoscope for those born in the year of the Snake is moving in a negative direction. It will result in unsmoothness. Obstacles will appear in your work and you will not feel refreshed. In your work, you will not cooperate. Therefore, if you encounter any incidents, you should resolve them with compromise. Do not express your emotions to those around you by speaking without thinking. Being calm, having good friendships, and using polite language when communicating with others will also help you get good results in return. During this period, your finances will be in a state of losing money. You should not gamble, speculate, or be greedy for wealth that does not belong to you. Do not lend money to others or act as guarantors. Do not do illegal business because a mistake will lead to prison.

As for your work, you will encounter chaos. Therefore, you should do more and speak less. Be careful of conflicts in your department. Be careful of unemployment. In terms of your family, there will be a lack of peace. You must be careful of conflicts from thoughtless words that will affect those close to you. You should also be careful of subordinates who will cause you trouble. In addition, you must be careful of accidents in the home and dangers from using tools that may cause injury or bleeding. This is another period when you must be careful of becoming a victim of fraud.

In terms of love, there will be a third party intervening, causing arguments due to misunderstandings. Do not go to entertainment venues that sell services.

Health is not good. Beware of liver disease, high blood pressure, food poisoning, and beware of accidents while traveling.

Support Days: 1 Jun., 5 Jun., 9 Jun., 13 Jun., 17 Jun., 21 Jun., 25 Jun., 29 Jun.

Lucky Days: 8 Jun., 20 Jun.
Misfortune Days: 11 Jun., 23 Jun.
Bad Days: 2 Jun., 14 Jun., 26 Jun.

Month 6 in the Snake Year (7 Jul 25 - 6 Aug 25)

This month, your horoscope shows a group of auspicious stars orbiting and shining brightly, so the auspicious light will cover your horoscope house. Your career will be smooth and your business will be successful. What you should do during this period is to set a plan for the whole year, check past mistakes to learn from them, and learn to adjust new things to accommodate current events. In addition, you should bring out projects that you have planned before along with methods to correct flaws. When the timing and opportunity are good during this period, you should put them into practice. Especially if the budget and manpower are ready, this time is the time that the sky is clear that you have been waiting for. If you are stuck with work or personal matters, you will receive good support and assistance. Starting a new job, or joining a joint venture, including various investments, is a good time for less risky investments. The results will be seen as beautiful income numbers.

This month, your finances are good. Cash flow will flow in from things you have invested and worked hard on. In terms of work, you will see progress. Business will be prosperous. Friends, relatives, customers, and business partners will all support you.

Your family is peaceful. Auspicious energy visits your home. There is a chance that you will organize an auspicious event inside the home. Otherwise, you will receive good news about the success of your family members.

In terms of love, this is a sweet time. For those who are single, this is a good opportunity to not be lonely. In addition, this month is a good time for asking for love, asking for a hand in marriage, getting engaged, or getting married.

For health, when your mind is healthy, your body will be healthy and free from diseases and parasites.

Support Days: 3 Jul., 7 Jul., 11 Jul., 15 Jul., 19 Jul., 23 Jul., 27 Jul., 31 Jul.
Lucky Days: 2 Jul., 14 Jul., 26 Jul.
Misfortune Days: 5 Jul., 17 Jul., 29 Jul.
Bad Days: 8 Jul., 20 Jul.

Month 7 in the Snake Year (7 Aug 25 - 6 Sep 25)

Your life path this month may be better, but the aftermath of the problem has not been completely solved. You should therefore quickly take this opportunity to make merit and create good deeds to enhance your charisma and destiny. What you should do during this time is to quickly start surgically removing the problem and not let the roots grow back. For those who work regularly, during this time, do not ask others to help you with your work. Otherwise, if the elders find out, you may be fined or punished to the point of unemployment.

Your work and business horoscope during this period will find a sponsor. Therefore, it is a good opportunity to seize this opportunity to push forward projects to increase your performance, generate sales, and expand your production base and customer base. Because the operations during this period will flow smoothly with both the elders helping to promote and the subordinates supporting. You can join forces in the same direction, which will increase your overall performance and increase your sales and income. In terms of starting a new job, entering into shares, and investing, it is time to wait and sing for now.

Your finances this month are moderate. Cash from your salary or products and services will flow normally. However, there is still some money from gambling to make you rich. However, you should limit your gambling.

Your family is smooth and happy. Make time for each other to be happier than before.

Sweet love is fulfilled. Those who are single have reached the stage where they have to make a decision. If you decide that it's right for you, you have to move forward quickly. If you wait too long, a good hand will snatch it away.

For those who are in a relationship, you may decide to ring the wedding bell during this period.

In terms of health, even though you are strong, you should be careful of injuries from sharp objects. Therefore, do not rush to the point of overlooking safety.

Support Days: 4 Aug., 8 Aug., 12 Aug., 16 Aug., 20 Aug., 24 Aug., 28 Aug.
Lucky Days: 7 Aug., 19 Aug., 31 Aug.
Misfortune Days: 10 Aug., 22 Aug.
Bad Days: 1 Aug., 13 Aug., 25 Aug.

Month 8 in the Snake Year (7 Sep 25 - 7 Oct 25)

This month, the path of life of the person will receive auspicious power from the shining stars, causing many activities that were not in order in the past to be concluded easily and smoothly this month. The job will progress and the business will find a prosperous place. On this occasion, what you should do is quickly clear up the pending work and seek new channels that others do not know much about. Open new markets for the future during the calm period. Also, you should analyze your strengths and weaknesses and know how to use the benefits of what you are good at in your work. In addition, you should be creative and present new things to make yourself a market leader.

For those who work regularly, you must not sit back and relax. Use your time to diligently increase your knowledge and new skills that are up-to-date with the times because, during this period of work, you will encounter new problems in waves. For investment this month, if the project is ready and you have enough money, you can invest.

This month's financial horoscope is prosperous. The person has a chance to expand. There is an auspicious time to open a business or open a new branch. For the family, this month is peaceful. You will have good news about fortune or there may be an auspicious event in the house. There will be an auspicious time to move into a new house marry a daughter-in-law or have more members. In terms of love blossoming, pointing at birds as birds, pointing at trees as trees.

As for health, it is moderate. Be careful about eating cold food or pickled food, it may be abnormal, affecting the stomach and intestines. In addition, be careful of accidents.

Support Days: 1 Sep., 5 Sep., 9 Sep., 13 Sep., 17 Sep., 21 Sep., 25 Sep., 29 Sep.
Lucky Days: 12 Sep., 24 Sep.
Misfortune Days: 3 Sep., 15 Sep., 27 Sep.
Bad Days: 6 Sep., 18 Sep., 30 Sep.

Month 9 in the Snake Year (8 Oct 25 - 6 Nov 25)

This month, your horoscope is stuck. Your life path has turned upside down again. Many activities and work are not smooth. Your work is not moving forward. The most important thing you should do during this period is to have your standpoint. Do not be fooled by invitations to go astray, which will lead to trouble. You should also control yourself well. Do not be greedy for ill-gotten wealth, because you may encounter a crisis of unemployment.

In addition, you must be careful of arguing and conflicts in your work. However, you should not compete with anyone. Just focus on your work and keep on adding knowledge and skills to your brain. This will pave the way for a good future. Even though your career and business direction are on the decline, if you are determined and do not give up, you will be able to change to an upward trend. If there is slander or backstabbing, you should avoid responding violently. Use your actions as proof instead. As for your work and investments, be careful not to be deceived this month.

Your financial luck this month is moderate. The money you receive may fluctuate. Gambling and taking risks will be high-risk. However, you should not be careless and spend lavishly. You should set aside some money for savings.

Your family horoscope at home is peaceful. But you should be careful with your relationship with your neighbors. Don't let your emotions get the better of you or even get physical. Relatives will argue. Be careful that talking too much will only cause harm. If you find out something, don't tell anyone else. You'll be safe.

In terms of love, you'll fall into a separation situation, so be careful that you don't have time for each other. It will make the other person feel abandoned. You need to manage your time well before it's too late. In terms of health, you won't have any illnesses.

Support Days: 3 Oct., 7 Oct., 11 Oct., 15 Oct., 19 Oct., 23 Oct., 27 Oct., 31 Oct.
Lucky Days: 6 Oct., 18 Oct., 30 Oct.
Misfortune Days: 9 Oct., 21 Oct.
Bad Days: 12 Oct., 24 Oct.

Month 10 in the Snake Year (7 Nov 25 - 6 Dec 25)

This month, your horoscope is moving to meet the evil stars. Your work and business must be planned carefully. There is an important thing that you should do during this period: any conflicts that can be discussed should be taken a step back. You should be mindful and control your emotions. In addition, you must carefully consider any documents or contracts during this period. Be careful of hidden secrets that will have negative effects later. In addition, you will likely encounter problems with account numbers that may be embellished and deceived, causing you to lose money. Be careful of problems with your subordinates that will bring trouble. Investments during this period are not good. You should put them on hold for now.

In terms of luck and finances, there is a chance of loss of money. You must be careful with your spending. During this period, you must not lend money to others. Do not sign financial guarantees. Do not invest in illegal or immoral businesses, including products that infringe copyrights. This month, even though your horoscope

The family will be wealthy. There will be good news about money, but good fortune comes with bad fortune. Therefore, you will lose money as well. Relatives and friends will encounter dangerous friends. Be careful of being accidentally hit or suffering from something you did not do, causing trouble.

In terms of love, it is moderate. If you want to keep your relationship sweet, you have to start by dividing your time more with your relationship.

In terms of health, it is not good. The person must be careful of liver disease, heart disease, and infectious diseases.

Support Days: 4 Nov., 8 Nov., 12 Nov., 16 Nov., 20 Nov., 24 Nov., 28 Nov.
Lucky Days: 11 Nov., 23 Nov.
Misfortune Days: 2 Nov., 14 Nov., 26 Nov.
Bad Days: 5 Nov., 17 Nov., 29 Nov.

Month 11 in the Snake Year (7 Dec 25 - 4 Jan 26)

In the last month of the year, your horoscope is moving to the destructive line, causing problems and obstacles to not ease. Also, be careful of the liquidity of the revolving fund which is quite stuck, and be careful of bad debts.

In terms of work or business, it is better to retreat than to advance because the market is turbulent. If you do not assess the situation well and rush forward, you can easily get hurt. During this period, you should stop grudges and reconcile with your enemies and competitors so that the situation does not get worse and you may have to face a double battle.

In terms of finances, direct income is uncertain. Avoid risky money and windfalls so that you do not get hurt. In addition, you should manage your work, finances, and people within your revolving fund capabilities. You should not create debts, whether short-term or long-term, during this period.

In terms of family, it is not very peaceful. Be careful of conflicts both inside and outside the home. There will be arguments and disagreements that will not yield to each other. Relatives and friends will have problems this month. Please do not love your friends more than yourself. If you take the blame, there will be endless problems with your family. Investments this month will cause more damage than profit. It is best to refrain for now.

In terms of love, you must be strong and stable during this period. Do not be shaken by those who instigate and avoid going to entertainment venues that will bring trouble.

In terms of health, even though you are strong, you must be careful of injuries from accidents.

Support Days: 2 Dec., 6 Dec., 10 Dec., 14 Dec., 18 Dec., 22 Dec., 26 Dec, 30 Dec.
Lucky Days: 5 Dec., 17 Dec., 29 Dec.
Misfortune Days: 8 Dec., 20 Dec.
Bad Days: 11 Dec., 23 Dec.

Amulet for The Year of the Snake
"Empress of Heaven (Mazu)"

Those born in the year of the Snake should set up and worship the sacred object "Empress of Heaven (Mazu)" to enhance their fortune. Place it on your work desk or cash desk to ask for her power and authority to protect and eliminate all misfortunes and bad luck so that the person can escape from suffering and distress, and receive only fortune, wealth, and auspicious things throughout the year.

In a chapter on advanced Feng Shui, it is mentioned that the deity who will descend to reside in the Mie Keng (house of destiny) of the year is a deity who can bring both good and bad fortune to the person of that year. Therefore, worshiping to enhance your fortune with a deity who descends to reside in the same year as your birth year is considered to have the best results and have the most impact on you. This is to rely on the power of that deity to help protect you while your fortune is declining and having bad luck to alleviate it. At the same time, ask for her blessing to help your business and trade go smoothly as desired, and bring glory and prosperity to you and your family.

Those born in the year of the Snake This year is considered a year of mixed good and bad fortune. Career and finances have almost no clear path. Although everything will gradually improve after July, I would like to warn you to be careful of friends who betray you. In terms of love, you should be the one to initiate if you want success, but it does not mean that you will find the right love to be your life partner this year. Those born in the year of the Snake or Mie Keng (the house of destiny) are in the Chi sign because your destiny this year has overlapped with your birth year, which is considered an offense to the Tai Sui god. In addition, many enemy stars are staring at you. This year is a year of mixed good and bad fortune. You will often encounter only hardship and suffering. Career and business have almost no clear path. Decisions to carry out various activities must be very careful and cautious to prevent mistakes and damage.

Financial fortune will cause you to lose unexpectedly. You should not hope for unexpected fortune and should not invest in businesses that are likely to be illegal, including copyright infringement. Because in addition to losing your wealth, you may also face criminal charges and tax expenses. You may also be dragged into conflicts. This year, I would like to warn you to be careful of friends who betray you. You must also be careful of accidents when traveling. You must also be careful of silent diseases that may appear to threaten you and make you anxious. In terms of love, you should be the one to initiate if you want your wish fulfilled. However, it does not mean that you will find the right love to be your life partner this year. If you want to eliminate and avoid bad luck, you should set up and worship the sacred object "Empress of Heaven (Mazu)" to ask for the power and authority of the goddess to help eliminate and eliminate bad luck, correct the destructive power of the evil stars and the clashing power of the year, promote good fortune, increase the wealth of the sacred place, and help the person of the horoscope to be healthy, have a peaceful and happy family, and be able to achieve what they hope for, experience wealth and happiness throughout the year. One of the most worshipped water gods in Asia is the "Empress of Heaven (Mazu)". According to her history, "Mazu" was born in Hokkien Province, Taiwan. She often helps people affected by water disasters, as well as helps villagers with their way of life and livelihood. She also helps relieve the suffering of villagers in terms of illness, thieves, deception, and various dangers. For those born in the year of the Snake, this year, their minds are often restless and they often have worries and worries. Therefore, worshiping the "Goddess of the Water" (Mazu), the goddess of the river, in addition to worshiping her to relieve suffering and danger, also helps create balance and will promote smooth work, business, and trade, and make money flow in. It helps relieve suffering and reduce seriousness to lightness so that all people born in the year of the Snake are happy.

In addition, those born in the year of the Snake should wear a lucky pendant of "Goddess of the Water" (Mazu) around their necks or carry it with them when traveling, whether near or far, so that the person will be filled with auspicious wealth and properties, and have prosperity and progress in both business and trade. The family will be peaceful and happy throughout the year, resulting in better and faster efficiency and effectiveness than before.

Good Direction: Southeast, Southwest, and West
Bad Direction: Northwest
Lucky Colors: Red, Pink, Orange, and Green.
Lucky Times: 09.00 – 10.59, 15.00 – 16.59, 17.00 – 18.59.
Bad Times: 03.00 – 04.59, 21.00 – 22.59.

Good Luck For 2025

15810741R00046